Let the Soul Slip Out

blue brooks

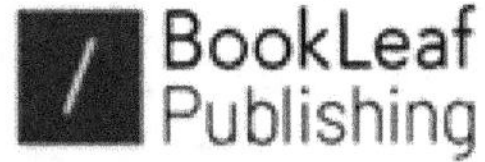

BookLeaf
Publishing

Presentation by *BookLeaf Publishing*

Web: www.bookleafpub.com

E-mail: info@bookleafpub.com

ISBN: 9789357210751

First edition 2022

DEDICATION

dedicated to you, who is reading this for a
reason

you beautiful soul - we are so lucky to have
you.

an experiment for lovers

1. locked in a room and told to describe one
another,
    the divine and the hellish and the in between,
    having been told the other will never know
    what they said

    1a. they know

untraceable

afraid of ascending above other bodies
bright light peeking through the holes in your
scalp

"birds of a feather flock together"
stuck between your wingspan and the next

caught in that space between time i know so
well-
old friends sat next to each other at a bar,
table with red velvet endcaps
and pink-rimmed, sparkly green nightcaps

scottish pearls shroud the floor and she realizes
if she wants to restring her necklace she'll just
have to lose a few

like moss

like a bundle of moss ripped from the earth
and a fist full of honeysuckles
trembling in your left hand,
clovers spilling out from behind your lips

bitterness ringing in your mouth like
metallic gunshot,
like blunt force trauma to the skull

sitting on the steps of the chapel
with your head in your hands
ushered out by some unseen force,

some spirit that haunts this place
too lonely to admit it needs someone
to haunt, to sit beside;
they call this spiritual suicide

the tongue catches everything -
even words
even heretics

draw a bath &soak in your sex

adulthood (responsibility) is doing what you
please
so long as you clean up after, washing
the blood down the drain, mopping
up your insides, waking
up for work sedated and dizzy

licking your fingertips
and staring into the mirror,
pretending this vessel isn't yours
because you know that two bodies
is the only solution
but you refused your other half

how does a body go missing?
an entire body, an entire experience?
are they not right here,
staring, walking closer and closer to the wall
leaning their weight into the plaster
hoping it will crack open to reveal a new room

strange joint

there is a strange comfort in collapsing
on a floor that is not yours
joints folding in on themselves
eyes forced upwards as if looking for god

upwards and upwards and upwards
caught in a cycle that ends in a
dismantling of direction;
disorientation and fingernails clicking against
quartz

through dizzy eyes and a syrup gaze,
thin lines of powder reflect against themselves
you think that you hear a scream
but it could just be the drugs

or the television

or a memory

woman in the screen

no symphony is as luscious as you
skin smears pink sweat
repulsive urge to drool drunk worship
ugly, raw, chanting,
delirious goddess of wax

the only lover the world has ever known
sprawled across the steps of a temple being born

out of body

let's fuck under the sun like the lights are off
this black mass creeping up my throat
and vomiting itself onto the grass of a new
spring

your hands, made of light,
wrapped around my neck like a band of gold
they are warm and i welcome the pressure
even if it means i am suffocating

"my heart is too heavy"
"what can't you carry? put something down"

and so i will rest my pain on your chest
and it will crush you with its weight
your spine flush with the earth,
eyes bulging wide with despair

remember what you told me?

"soon it will not matter. soon this moment will
not exist."
"soon you will be released from the clutches of
this barren earth"

but she is not barren!
she is overflowing and bountiful,
your eyes just aren't wide enough to see her all
at once;
your hair is falling over your lids,
a spot in your vision

i am seeing you more clearly now -
with every memory i lie on your ribs
i am running out of room now
so i rest the smaller pains along your shins
and they trace your body like the outlines
that clutter murder scenes

maybe this was one;
murdering myself because i have outgrown her.

"why don't you write anymore?"
"it hurts"
"your heart?"
"no, my hands"

liminal space

i don't care where i am
as long as it feels good

slouched against the wall
at the train station,
in the backseat of an escalade
while she's throwing up
riding shotgun,
thrown across the kitchen floor,
cross-eyed & hazy-faced

it's nothing but a sword,
blade buried deep beneath flesh
all the way up to the crystals

smackboy

jumping out of my bones,
leaving you space to fill
between the holes in the marrow

spongy and wet like after dinner
hands sinking into rising water,
hot foam seeping in to each block of flesh

folded hands, twisting wrists to show god
what you've done -
sacrificing yourself to the gods but forgetting
that you have to do the killing yourself
you're the only one here and god,
with all of the powers she does have,
cannot kill you for her

here is when you stop writing because it is
painful to want to say:
"you beat your head into submission, two fists
against skull,
and the blood comes out in rivers,
pouring over the valleys,
resting beneath the soil,
an untapped reservoir of re-creation"

you are your eyes,
your heart,
the meat of your palm,
all of your flesh
and all that it contains

bent over backwards
to an infinity of mirrors
glaring back, lovingly
the same motion carried
out in every single one

blood orange

when it stormed we were forced to line up
outside with
pieces of an orange in our mouths,
told not to devour the delicate

fruit teaching us to cradle each of our words
as if life depends on them,
because it does

and now you put me down
on the side of the road
a bullet through my brain
like a dog gone rabid

you watch my teeth sink into sand
and fold up the rearview
no chance for a glance

blood orange still wasting away
resting on my tongue, never pierced
and never loved

black swan

starving women
eating fire to keep ourselves warm

born on wire
shaping us into perfect form

building up our own walls
until all we want to do
is leap over them

some things to recall:

* the human condition is chronic - we are time
encapsulated,the expansion of the universe held
within our form

* the body is the site of the mind, the mind is
contained;
your mind is in your chest, the bullets shoot you
dead

* the body is a liminal space in which time does
not "pass" -time stands still within us; we are
transitory specimens

* your soul is not trapped - it is being protected -
housed;your soul is happening to you

time travel

my fingers trace the grain of the wood
in front of me, turning it into flesh

this is what i am thinking of when i look away -
a body that can't keep itself warm anymore

a body spilling out of itself

a body that once held someone inside of it

a body that let the soul slip out

arson

i burned the bed we
used to sleep on. i hope you
felt that in your chest

angels are forged by fire

so here i am, at the top of the stairs.

a smooth, glistening layer of blood settled over
the grain of the oak beneath. if steps could speak
they would sound like smoke; sultry and
obsessive. if they could look it would hurt. bare
feet glazing the surface, i must look like jesus
standing here. i must look like the virgin mary in
the dreams of the prophet. i must be due for a
good collapsing, hair crusted with red droplets
and body limp in the mess.

here i am now, staring down at the level beneath
me, afraid to ripple the thickness that i am
standing so solidly in. there is no blood where
my flesh meets mahogany and so i have a grip
on the floorboards - but should i move, i know in
my guts that i will slip and drown.

how do i know the blood has a bottom? how do i
know it understands mercy, compassion? it is
life, and yet it is so cruel. i've seen it spill out of
veins before, blue tunnels shooting out the
stream that breathes, across whatever is beneath,
god forbid. i stand here, paralyzed and probably

contracting something, staring at the beautiful
things around me and afraid to mix tears with
what is below.

water and blood, like water and oil. nothing
mixes anymore. absolutely nothing. i accept that
i will remain like this until my legs give out.

and then my legs have broken on me, dropping
me closer to hell than i would ever willingly be.
my shins, they're soaking. i was supposed to
write about a place i felt safe in and i am
recognizing now that i am always safe, even
when i am not. my soul is safe i think because it
is somewhere else.

i grip the cast iron gate (bent to all heaven) that
surrounds saint joseph's and god all i want is
water. i grip the bars until they bend, until my
bone is also It. until i cry over the grass because
mixing water and life is okay sometimes, so long
as the life is diluted. blood would be too pure,
but soil can handle my sadness. it sucks it up and
transmutes every jolt of pain into a "blade" of
grass.

how fitting; anger cannot exist without pain and
here is the defense. here is the protection, cutting
up through the dirt and slicing its way toward

the sky. grass thinks it will become a tree, and trees think they will become bigger trees. we're all being fooled. well, maybe we aren't being fooled; we are just fools.

i break the stained glass with the ripples in the blood i am soaking in. the shockwaves shake the frame. the shards fall onto the organ, heavy enough to play notes through the chambers of the church. (a building, is what it is, really. we are the churches. churches inside of buildings we call churches. abhorrent.) and what plays drowns out this disgusting notion that a human being is something that should actively worship anything but itself. it is so beautiful that we forget.

i forget where i was, looking in the mirror, eyes stationary while my head sways from side to side, yellow irises reflecting off the shimmering light of the burning, burning, burning star resting against the window pane. a synagogue is so much more comforting. i wonder if anyone will notice that my eyes are yellow. because they are, they're gold.

i know this because a priest smacked my mouth after seeing my eyes, insisting them to be a sign of the devil. that i must have witches surrounding me on the Other Side. that angels find it difficult to reach me. the same man that when i asked, "if god created everything, what created god?", he swung his open fist into my jaw. "god is all there ever was and all there ever will be".

in a metaphysical shop once, a shaman asked my mother, "she doesn't like mirrors, does she?"

i was so afraid he could see my soul. i was so afraid he would see me for who i am. for who he was, reflected off of me. he told her i needed to protect myself. that i needed help and that he knew why i was here. i don't want to know why i am here. i would like to continue thinking that i am here to exist, and then to simply leave. i want to leave nothing behind, i want it to all come with me, always, and i am so goddamn afraid of not being able to take myself along into the next place i should end up. i think that maybe i am afraid of ever even going.

string theory

tie a knot around your finger and you'll
rememberall the things you thought
you could never forget

every experience is
life-changing

the pulsing of sex,
that red light illuminating clouded glass

ivy hanging from roots buried in your scalp
breath sliding out of gullet,
surely, completely, continuously

thought form struggling to escape
underwater and drowning in the rain
soaking up the fresh water and leaving behind
poison

shamrock

luck hangs like a chandelier
over ballroom drenched in sweet red wine

dilapidated billboard reminds us we're home;
the world looks so real from inside your youth

desire path

i think that when you die you fall through the
cracks of time, reliving it all at once, completely
and helplessly suspended between the illusion of
death and the human recklessness that causes us
to believe in living,

paralyzed in a prayer for a lover that won't leave
marks when they bite, won't leave fingerprints
smudged around the edges of the frame you live
in, with hands that admire what eyes can't feel

this is your body, until you die
and probably even after that

www.ingramcontent.com/pod-product-compliance
Lightning Source LLC
La Vergne TN
LVHW051248200726
843510LV00011B/1747